REDEMPTION BRIDGE

My story of addiction
and
recovery

CHRIS FORESTA

ISBN- 978-1-7374495-0-8

Table of Contents

Foreword

I remember meeting Chris many years ago. His heroin addiction had ravaged him emotionally and physically. He had lost everything: his marriage, his job, personal possessions, and even his car. This story is gripping and true. It's a story of addiction and how it can take you to the darkest of darkest places. But it is also a story of inspiration and of much hope and healing. That recovery and long-term sobriety is real, even for someone in Chris's situation.

They say addiction is a disease. I learned from personal experience that this statement is true. My two oldest boys struggled with a heroin addiction years ago just like Chris. The Renaissance Ranch Treatment Center helped us understand that people who are addicted are not bad people needing to be good; they are sick people needing help. The story of Chris in his trials with an addiction is real and all too common. Many have been where Chris is, where there is no hope, on the edge of living or dying, living in numb desperation, and thinking there's no hope. But there is hope. There is hope with the 12 steps of recovery. There is hope in our Savior Jesus Christ and in the healing power of his atoning sacrifice. There is hope that a person can heal and recover from addiction.

Many times, addiction seems hopeless. If you are struggling with an addiction or you know somebody who is and you feel hopeless, this book will inspire you and bring you comfort. Chris's experience of hopelessness and suicidal tendencies is real. Drug addiction takes a person to the bottom of the bottom. But there is a way out.

Now as an owner of the Renaissance Ranch, and after seeing many addicts find long term recovery, I've learned that there's true hope and healing. Through the 12 steps and with the help of a higher power, we have seen hundreds recover and get their lives back. This book will help you on your journey and learn about the dark abyss of addiction, but also, the great hope and healing that can truly take place for you and your family. This book is a must-read, particularly if you or one of your family members or friends are struggling with addiction. It will inspire you and bring peace to your heart!

~ Rick Dixon
Renaissance Ranch Treatment Centers

PART 1

Chapter 1

A Mind Full of Intervention

On May 2nd, 2013, Gary Free suddenly sat up in bed at 2:00 a.m. with an unexpected, imposing thought urging him to visit me in Las Vegas, Nevada. This was peculiar because at that time, my uncle and I barely knew each other. Nevertheless, the powerful feeling that motivated him to act that morning likely saved my life.

Gary is an early riser; he usually gets out of bed before his alarm clock goes off. As soon as his feet hit the carpet that morning, he decided to scrap all plans for the day and drive to Las Vegas. As his wife walked by him, he slightly dawdled before committing to the first words he would speak that day.

"Kathy, I need to go visit my nephew, Chris. I'm driving to Las Vegas today."

They both knew I was struggling with addiction because they had tried to help me get into treatment about six months prior.

"What?" she responded with a nonplussed look on her face.

My aunt is used to Gary's spontaneity and how decisively he changes plans if he feels something is extremely important, so the look of bewilderment she wore faded quickly - her demeanor shifting to an attitude of radical acceptance.

I had missed my Grandma's funeral in Salt Lake the previous winter, and when Gary realized it, he asked my mom, "Carolyn, how is Chris doing? It doesn't seem like him to miss Mom's funeral." He asked with genuine concern and sincerity and was right to assume something wasn't right. All of Grandma's grandchildren were very close to her, and I was no exception. My mom's face was despairing as she diffidently responded, clenching down her jaw muscles as her eyes swelled and tears trickled down her cold, rosy cheeks.

"Gary, Chris is addicted to heroin. He lost his job and I think he has just given up on everything. I don't know what to do." She was inconsolably crying now.

Her mother had just died, and as she watched her other two sons with Gary's boys carry the coffin where Grandma Free now rested, she couldn't help imagining my body in there.

The thought of her firstborn son passing away from a drug overdose made her shudder.

I was regularly using dangerously potent drugs and living off unemployment in a converted studio garage located just a few houses down from the house my parents raised us in as children before their divorce in 2000. The neighborhood had aged a lot. The houses all looked much older, and the landscaping was unkempt and overgrown in most of the yards. The demographic was also different as Spring Valley became more central during the housing boom leading up to the Great Recession.

I secretly hoped I wouldn't wake up in the morning every time I nodded out at night. "Nodding" is a slang term used when someone is so high, they fall in and out of consciousness. It's not sleeping, although it can appear that way. In my opinion, opioids do a much better job of numbing emotional pain than they do physical pain. They are, quite literally, a numbing composition.

Perhaps the reason they work so well for serious, painful injuries is the brain sends a message telling your mind and body that you don't care about the pain anymore, even though it has not gone away. The message it always sent my body was that I didn't need to care about anything or any kind of pain anymore.

If I had some "Black" or "H," both street code for black tar heroin, depending on the city you buy it in, I could forget my problems, even if it was only for a few hours. I'd stop despondently thinking about my ex-wife sleeping with a friend I had foolishly rented a room to amid my progressing addiction, back when my life was just getting to the point where everything was about to collapse. I was completely enslaved and powerless to prevent my inevitable demise now, and my mom was right. I had given up. I had lost everything and no longer had a purpose. I had nothing to live for anymore.

About six months passed by with very little communication to friends and family. The first attempt at intervention was unsuccessful, and my mom was mentally preparing herself for another funeral - my funeral. I had no idea my uncle was on his way, ready to help me "grab the bull by the horns" as he would say. He was now totally dedicated to this mission, driving southbound on I-15 on a brisk, sunny morning in May of 2013. As he grabbed his phone to call my mom for an address, he was flabbergasted to see I responded to an old text message he had sent a few weeks prior. My text was sent about 30 minutes after he awoke to that feeling urging him to visit Las Vegas.

"What a strange coincidence," he thought to himself as he accelerated, now driving south of

Beaver where the speed limit increases to 80 mph.

Gary (4/19/2013)-Hi Chris how are you doing? I might come see you sometime.

Chris-(5/2/2013) That would be good Uncle Gary, I am not doing too well.

I had taken a massive amount of Xanax and mixed it with some really strong Black that previous night, fully aware the deadly concoction could provoke an overdose with irreversible consequences. That afternoon, Gary arrived with my brother, Tony, and my mom. I obviously assumed my late-night text had prompted Gary's surprise visit, but he didn't even see it until he was already enroute.

They asked me if I was high or if I had been using drugs. I didn't hesitate in my answer, quickly admitting I needed help and inviting them inside the dark, windowless cavern in which I resided. I didn't even hide the tin foils blackened with the residue of heroin I had smoked just moments before they arrived. I wanted them to see how bad it was because it was a cry for help. I knew I was sick. They could see I was dying, but somehow all three of them still believed there was hope. Tony is my youngest sibling; he and I are both musicians. He led a very successful band for many years and is admittedly much more musically gifted than I.

"Chris, please don't die with music still inside you," he said. I realize now the hidden allegorical meaning in little Tony's advice, and I often think back on how those words inspired me to change in the early stages of my recovery.

When addicts change their lives, each has so much to give back to the world. There is so much wisdom in the hearts and minds of men and women willing to fight, who are armed to win this battle every day. These men and women beat odds year after year, inspiring and helping others to change their lives, altering the disproportionate and unfortunate reality of those odds.

I always tried to save myself at least a small portion of Black for the next day to relieve the painful withdrawals that were always just eight short hours away, but I never could. If you have ever been addicted to heroin, you know just how futile any attempt at conservation is. I woke in the afternoons, barely able to muster up enough strength to take my dog out front so he could relieve himself.

One time I tried to explain to this small, well-trained Basenji mutt that he had permission to poop on the floor so I didn't have to get up and go outside. He didn't get it. I remember thinking to myself, "He'll have to hold it because I'm too sick to get out of bed." That is how selfish this disease can make a person. It's no wonder the addict population has been collectively misunderstood for so long by society. The hurtful things we do to the people and others we love most are almost as devastating as the damage we do to ourselves.

Withdrawal symptoms caused my depression to be so intense that I sometimes just cried for hours, shivering and shaking, unable to get comfortable in a pool of my own sweat. I was pleading to the Dope Man to visit my home first when he made his rounds that day. Until I got high, I would be trapped in my head and tormented by events leading me to this point in my life. My 15-year-long career with Expedia was ruined and my first marriage had ended in a scandal. I had lost my home and wrecked my car. My only acquaintances were other men and women also addicted to heroin, people with no hope and nothing to lose, people that I meant nothing to and who meant nothing to me.

Because I was obsessed with heroin, there was no one left in my life I cared about except my dog, Rody. He was my only friend. Only a few people had faith that I could beat this illness, and believe me, neither Rody nor I was one of them. Gary Free was, and lucky for me, he is a patiently optimistic man.

Chapter 2

The Free's

Ten years ago, I would never have imagined myself ending up in Salt Lake City as a Christian and a member of The Church of Jesus Christ of Latter-day Saints. I admit I admired the way my mom's large, extended family, which resided in the east suburb of Sandy, Utah, was always so full of joy, carefully upholding a high standard of morality and integrity as members of the church. When I was a child, I looked forward to visiting and participating in family meals and activities with my cousins during visits to the Salt Lake valley.

My younger brothers and I were always welcomed and included in the festivities, and the adults there didn't need to drink alcohol to turn a party into a good time. In fact, they didn't drink at all. My dad would walk up the hill where Gary's three-story house was built when he needed to go smoke, out of sight from the children. My mother and father always showed approbation for the values Gary and Kathy taught their children. To this day, they both have the utmost respect for my aunt and uncle, and for everything they have accomplished. Gary and Kathy Free are the most guided people I have ever known.

Once their children all moved out to start families of their own, the Frees relocated from Sandy to Draper as empty nesters, building a large, custom home at the base of the Traverse Mountains. It's spacious enough to host Sunday get-togethers for a growing family of five living children and twenty grandchildren. Gary is an entrepreneur and philanthropist with a reputation for being honest, demonstrating pure integrity in all his affairs. He and Kathy have more than they show, because flashing expensive worldly possessions in public couldn't be a less important priority to them. When Gary does spend money on himself, it's for race cars he can legally drive at speeds exceeding 150 miles an hour around a track, or an ATV he can use to climb the side of a mountain at a 75-degree angle.

It's a good thing my uncle always kept both of his hands firmly planted on the "Iron Rod" because he'd likely have become addicted to something terrible if he'd ever let go. Risk takers like Gary have a more fulfilling life experience than many, but there is a fine line between taking risks and making poor choices. My aunt and uncle are very calculated people; they have always applied conservative values in their lives, prayerfully considering financial decisions before executing them. They got married at a young age with barely a dime to their names, both coming from humble beginnings. Gary graduated college with a degree in business, and today his net worth is in the same tax bracket as many popular movie stars and famous musicians. The irony is that he and Kathy don't care about vain recognition. They would be just as happy as members of the middle-class. The only downside for them would be making fewer donations to their various charitable endeavors.

When I was eight years old, Gary baptized me into the religion he and my mother were raised in. I remember Grandma Free being so proud of me and writing a letter to me in my scriptures about what baptism meant to her. She promised that God would guide me through life and help me make the right choices if I was willing to listen to His promptings.

As I got older, I developed an atheistic creed and was quick to criticize Christians. I coerced religious people into debates to feed my ego, which regretfully only hardened my heart and the hearts of those victim to my condescending nature. I was a jerk and a know-it-all back then. I can admit that now because it doesn't bother me anymore to say I was wrong.

As a teenager who recklessly, secretly, and meticulously used drugs and alcohol, I often opened the set of scriptures where my Grandma had written those words, and the loving advice she gave to me as a child would bring me so much peace. These are my first memories of feeling a peaceful spirit as a teenager who was about to embark on a dark and dangerous journey, ultimately losing my way in a wilderness of horrors. Even the exceptionally spiritually fortified Gary had no idea how long the trip back would take.

Chapter 3

Renaissance Ranch

G ary had already done the legwork to find a drug treatment center close to his home in Draper. He learned about a place called Renaissance Ranch located in Bluffdale, Utah, just south of Salt Lake City, from a member of his ward whose sons went through the program several years before I did. The male-only facility was founded and run by H.R. Brown, a recovering addict with many years of continued sobriety. He is a man of God with a rock-solid testimony of his Mormon faith. He is very smart, and I was confounded that someone so articulate and intelligent could subscribe to what seemed to be a farfetched doctrine. What baffled me more is that he had willingly converted as an adult, which threw my initial theory of brainwashing through childhood indoctrination out the window. "HR" unapologetically referred to the Ranch as the "LDS Treatment Program."

On the day of my intake in May of 2013, I remember thinking to myself, "These people are all a bunch of religious Christian nutcases who talk to an imaginary, made-up god and foolishly believe that he is the solution to this problem. There is no way this place can help me!"

The Ranch is a 9,000 square-foot colonial style mansion, with large columns rising three stories high, sitting on three acres of ranch land. There are panoramic views of the Wasatch mountains just over the horizon, past the quarter-mile-long oval running track where a horse stable sits to the eastern front of the residence's long, narrow porch. As I turned around for one last look before ringing the doorbell, I said to my mother, "I will just make the best of it, and use the time to get this addiction thing out of my system. At least it's a nice place, plus they said we will be doing a lot of hiking, so I can get back in shape."

Looking back, I realize most of the early assumptions I made about the Ranch were wrong, much like the assumptions I made about why I had developed a bad habit of inhaling heroin off tin foil slabs through hollowed out Bic pens. There was nothing in the curriculum mandating that I read scriptures, attend church meetings, or anything else that could be an attempt to "force me to become a Mormon." We did pray before meals, but the person saying it did so voluntarily.

The interior was peppered with Christian art and LDS imagery, which I at first balked at. But in the weeks ahead, those pictures would bring me serenity and inner peace when I found myself staring off into them. I wouldn't admit that back then, of course, still a proud atheist and more lost than I could have possibly known in those first few weeks of treatment.

Once I completed the intake and was officially checked in, I was introduced to the 20 men busy doing dishes and mopping the large dinner hall where they had just finished eating a family style dinner. The food there was terrific. One of the residents offered me a plate, but I couldn't eat very much the first few days. I was fresh out of detox, overwhelmed, and intimidated by the roaring sounds of laughter and conversation going on all around me. Some of the guys were giving hugs as they introduced themselves, and nearly all of them spoke the words, "I am glad you are here," which is a tradition at the Ranch. Over time, I would come to realize that most, if not all of them, really meant it. Within a few weeks, I was hugging newcomers brave enough to walk through those doors and confront themselves, men with little hope, appearing just as defeated as I did my first day.

I'd say, "I am glad you are here, bro. You are in the right place."

We followed a rigid schedule, intentionally designed to keep us busy and active. An idle mind is the devil's playground, and the architects of the Ranch's program are very aware of that. If you are going to go into your head, it's best to take someone with you, someone who can guide you through your past and help you process any events that bring to the surface emotions you didn't realize had been burnt in your subconscious, repressed but not forgotten.

Every day of the week except for the Sabbath, our alarm clocks went off at 6:00 a.m. I had to have my bed made within the first 10 minutes of rising in the morning per the contract every admit signs at the time of their intake. Residents are required to follow many rules to be successful at the Ranch, but there is a good reason for them all, although most didn't make any sense to me at first. I hadn't awakened that early since I was in high school. Hating the mornings already made it hard. I was required to get up in the acute, post-withdrawal stage of recovery which lasted for a few weeks. And then there were the more minor symptoms which lasted for many months.

Once beds were made, we met in the front corridor at the bottom of two identical spiral staircases which outwardly curved in opposite directions, leading to the upstairs bedrooms. We did a quick attendance check, then headed outside to complete the mandatory mile-long walk – four laps around a large, oval-shaped track which stretched around a field of grass where we sometimes played sports during recreation time. We looked like a mob of mindless zombies in pajamas aimlessly following each other in circles with no people to eat because the rest of Bluffdale hadn't yet awakened. Most of us were still half asleep, our faces garbed in morning scowls. I literally had to drag myself to the finish line at first; a few times I was close to throwing up and quitting. As other guys effortlessly lapped me, I told myself, "You are in the wrong place, Chris. You can't do this. You are in treatment with a bunch of Mormon Boy Scouts who were probably active and fit the day they arrived. But you are a mess."

These assumptions turned out to be untrue. I was more like these guys than I realized.

After the walk, we split into two smaller groups and met in the basement living space, just outside a room I shared with a dude named Matt P. His snoring sounded like he was standing next to me violently sawing through giant logs. That first night. I impetuously began slamming drawers at around 3:00 a.m. to try to wake up him up. My plan was to quickly fall asleep in the fleeting five-minute window it would take before the tormenting noise resumed.

"I'm pretty sure he's going to consume all the oxygen in our room within a few minutes anyway, mercifully killing us both," I'd think to myself as the repetition grew louder every time he inhaled.

We'd both laugh about this later, of course. Matt is a good man. Today he is a House Manager at the Ranch. The penalty for an alumnus who relapses after treatment should be to share a room in the basement with Matt for a night.

The early morning 6:50 a.m. group was the first of several mandatory group meetings that took place throughout the day, Monday through Friday, when the clinical staff was present. We'd read from the Big Book of Alcoholics Anonymous, then present homework assignments we'd have to handwrite because electronic devices, including cell phones and computers, were strictly prohibited to protect anonymity. After every group, we huddled up, bowed our tired heads, and said the Serenity Prayer, *"God, Grant me the serenity to accept the things I cannot change, courage to change the things I can, and the wisdom to know the difference."* It's common for this prayer to be repeated after meetings of Alcoholics Anonymous, Narcotics Anonymous, and Cocaine Anonymous.

The sun was up by then, and we had about 45 minutes before meeting for breakfast where, for the first time of the day, we'd have any staff supervision. Brian H, the House Manager, would be in the kitchen frying eggs and hash browns, usually playing a hipster song through a speaker connected to his phone set on the center island counter which had bar chairs that spun from side to side snugly attached around it.

Brian had been clean for many years, and I admired how seriously he took Recovery—not just his own, but ours too. The glasses covering his eyes gave a first impression that he was a brainy, discerning person. But this was not untrue. He always had valuable insights to add to the group conversation, and he did so with little intensity, carefully considering his words before presenting them. I remember he once said, "It's a simple program. You just get up, get out of bed, and start doing things."

In hindsight, it was a simple program, but it didn't feel simple at first. Nothing in my life felt simple. Still, there is a lot of wisdom in those words. Motivation and willingness are where Recovery starts, and the Ranch's simple program was the start of mine.

The residence was lavishly furnished with plush sofas in the common areas adding to a tranquil setting for the Therapeutic Community or "TC" meetings we attended twice daily. At first, it seemed like a pointless waste of time, an outlet for whining, complaining, and "ratting each other out" as my secretive Sicilian father would say. We were responsible for holding ourselves and each other accountable for breaking rules and exhibiting addictive behaviors that are not conducive to the values one must uphold to be successful in Recovery. It also gave everyone in the room an opportunity to nip brewing resentments toward each other in the bud before they escalated to name-calling or something worse.

I remember thinking to myself, "Man, this is an uncomfortable experience. Why do we have to do this?" Just as it seemed the meeting was about to end, Brian answered the question I just asked myself in my mind seconds before.

He said, "Guys, if you are comfortable over the next few months, you are not doing this program right."

Suddenly, it felt like a crane dropped a ton of bricks on my chest as I realized the next words uttered by Nick L, a stocky man who was clearly a former high school football player and jock, were directed at me. "Chris, I have some resentments and some things to call you out on. You have to shower every morning, bro. You also only did three laps this morning."

I felt like a target of heavy artillery coming from all sides as another said, "Yeah, Chris, you are always laying around on the couches after the morning meetings. That's against the rules, bro."

One by one, the group laid into me.

I stormed out of the room. Enraged and embarrassed, I headed down to my basement sleeping quarters and began to pack my bags. What I didn't know then is that the group does this to any of the brothers who are falling behind, much like a soldier motivates the guy next to him in a foxhole to keep fighting and forget about the pain and fear for the moment. We are only as strong as our weakest link, and in a household full of drug addicts and alcoholics, bad behaviors spread like cancer if they are not addressed immediately. I hated everyone there at first. But for the first time in my life, I had friends that were going to call out my crap and hold me accountable.

Some of the guys that called me out the most ended up becoming lifelong friends. One of them would share the foxhole with me for many years after our stay at the Ranch. Taylor R is a tall, handsome man with an athletic build and a recklessly passionate drive to win everything. He's about seven years younger than me. Back then, his meth addiction had thinned him so much that his sucked-in face and exposed jaw line gave him the appearance of a malnourished Ethiopian refugee with albinism. There was a drab pessimism every time he shared his feelings in group, and I felt he was always taking everything way too seriously. Sometimes in the TC meeting, when my mind wandered, I entertainingly pictured Taylor so angry that his head exploded. He and I made it a daily priority to spitefully call each other out, intentionally trying to piss each other off. One time I picked at him so purposefully that he hit a wall with his fist, knocking a picture off it. It made me shudder, and I was admittedly filled with guilt as it came crashing down.

There were only two things that he and I had in common in those first weeks. We were both drug addicts, and we both shared basement rooms with men who sounded like wart hogs when they slept. Around 10:30 p.m., we grudgingly met each other in the basement living room, each of us carrying a pillow and a blanket, bound for two large couches situated perpendicularly in the shape of an L. Taylor had his scriptures in one hand, and blanket and pillow in the other. He epitomized everything I hated about religion. After a few nights, I broke our uncomfortable silence by mockingly asking him to read the Book of Mormon out loud. Taylor is smart; he knew what I was doing. But he wasn't going to squander an opportunity to soften my heart, even at the risk of eliciting a patronizing response. He began to read from Alma 32:28-33:

28 Now, we will compare the word unto a seed. Now, if ye give place, that a seed may be planted in your heart, behold, if it be a true seed, or a good seed, if ye do not cast it out by your unbelief, that ye will resist the Spirit of the Lord, behold, it will begin to swell within your breasts; and when you feel these swelling motions, ye will begin to say within yourselves—It must needs be that this is a good seed, or that the word is good, for it beginneth to enlarge my soul; yea, it beginneth to enlighten my understanding, yea, it beginneth to be delicious to me.

29 Now behold, would not this increase your faith? I say unto you, Yea; nevertheless it hath not grown up to a perfect knowledge.

30 But behold, as the seed swelleth, and sprouteth, and beginneth to grow, then you must needs say that the seed is good; for behold it swelleth, and sprouteth, and beginneth to grow. And now, behold, will not this strengthen your faith? Yea, it will strengthen your faith: for ye will say I know that this is a good seed; for behold it sprouteth and beginneth to grow.

31 And now, behold, are ye sure that this is a good seed? I say unto you, Yea; for every seed bringeth forth unto its own likeness.

32 Therefore, if a seed groweth it is good, but if it groweth not, behold it is not good, therefore it is cast away.

33 And now, behold, because ye have tried the experiment, and planted the seed, and it swelleth and sprouteth, and beginneth to grow, ye must needs know that the seed is good.

Something about Alma's words struck me dumb. The seed was planted in my heart that night. It was planted by a foe who would become one of my best friends in the months and years to come. I was willing to try the experiment Alma talked about, because the seed was planted. It was planted by Taylor, and I am forever grateful to him for following his heart and doing that.

Chapter 4

The Scorpion on My Head

Kris Groves runs the clinical team at the Ranch. She is the only female presence in the all-male residence. When we were introduced, I had already been fed a contradictory blend of suggestions describing her character, as well as some disapproving rants by the newer intakes about her approach to treating substance abuse clients. Kris was always modestly dressed in Sunday clothes, and carried her slightly overweight shape with a self-assurance as if she was telling the world she loved herself the way she was, as everyone should. I was one of the many men who at first mistakenly assumed she was a haughty, man-hating tyrant who enjoyed tearing us down and making us feel stupid whenever an opportunity presented itself.

We assembled for meetings in the mornings and afternoons, and the groups Kris facilitated were led with intensity, deliberately attempting to temper the destructive male ego which I eventually learned was the source of my many character flaws.

"Do you guys know that your ego wants to kill you?" she'd say, squinting her eyes as she threw her mouth wide open in disgust. "You may think I am picking on you, but I'm not. I'm attacking your narcissistic, prideful ego. If you had a scorpion on your head that was about to sting you, I'd smack you as hard as possible to knock it off before you were killed."

I still didn't like her yet, but I had to admit she was starting to make sense. Another hallmark expression Kris often exhibited was her sardonic pout, worn when she craftily exposed sensitivity in the manliest of men determined to resist her tear-forming enchantments.

"I know it hurts, but guys, you have to feel it to heal it," she cleverly declared, putting her hand over her heart and fixing her eyes upon the group. Her spinning gaze eventually landed on me as she leaned forward in her chair, turning a pen in her other hand.

"How are you feeling this morning, Chris? Do you want talk about anything today?" she sympathetically asked as I struggled to compose myself enough to respond with a convincing, "Nope, I am fine, but thanks for asking."

It seemed like hours went by as she tolerantly considered my short response, examining my behavior with a playfully curious expression on her face. Shifting her head into a tilted position, she resumed her line of inquiry, "Well, you are in rehab, so I wonder how fine you could possibly be, considering you just got out of detox. So why are you here, Chris, if you are fine?"

Annoyed by what I felt was a patronizing question with an obvious answer, I aloofly responded, with growing contempt in my tone, "Well, clearly because I am a heroin addict. I have a drug problem, Kris. That's why I am here, but you are the therapist. Why don't you tell me?"

Unfazed by my retaliatory response and derisive posturing, she quickly countered, "Okay, let me see if I can help. Why are you a heroin addict? Did you start using the deadliest illegal drugs you could find because you were sick of feeling happy and decided that numbing out sounded more appealing?"

Sensing the rhetorical nature of her question, I paused, giving her a chance to answer it herself.

"You started numbing because you couldn't stand the feelings of shame and regret anymore, right?" Again, without answering, I let her continue her train of thought, now respectfully giving her my full attention.

"I don't think drugs are your problem at all, Chris. I think drugs are your solution." I only had to ponder those words for a few seconds before I realized the sensibility in her wisdom. Drugs and alcohol were never my problem. They were my solution, albeit not a very good one, but the best one I could come up with at the time.

In the weeks to come, Kris slowly peeled away at my defense mechanisms as if they were layers of an onion, helping me realize that blaming people, places, and institutions for my problems was keeping me sick. She wasn't going to coddle me, but just as fiercely, as she pointed out my faults, she encouraged me to accept and forgive myself for events that I did not cause, fostering reconciliation for traumatic childhood experiences that shouldn't have happened but did because the world is not perfect.

I was willing to become vulnerable in one-on-one meetings with her, openly expressing feelings I wasn't comfortable exposing in groups. In one of our last sessions, she introduced me to a concept that transformed my understanding of addiction.

"Do you want to know what the root of all addiction is, Chris?" she asked with an outgoing smile and an outward expression, signifying she now considered us friends, not just a counselor and her client. "It's shame. We feel shame because we are taught to."

I playfully and sarcastically responded, "So, my mom and dad shamed me into becoming a drug addict? I knew it!"

She chuckled, almost as if she was expecting me to make a joke. "No, but it is a family disease, Chris." After pausing for a few seconds, she swiftly changed the subject as if she just remembered something of incredible importance.

"By the way, Brian complimented you on how much progress you have made. But he mentioned you are still not calling the new guys out when they break rules. What's up with that?"

I responded, declaratively and with conviction, "Because I don't rat people out, Kris. There is nothing lower than a rat."

I could see now she was doing a mind-ninja trick on me by changing the topic from before, masterfully circling back to drive her point home. "Hmm, I'm guessing your father taught you that. Tell me more about him," she said, sitting back in her chair with her hand over her heart and forming a sarcastic pout with her lips.

Chapter 5

Growing up Italian

In 1979, my mother and father were co-workers for the Stardust Hotel and Casino, located on the south end of Las Vegas Boulevard, during a phase in the city's history when Italian and Jewish gangsters were in charge. My mother, born Carolyn Janet Free, had dropped out of college and fled from her home in Salt Lake City. She sought a life free from conformity and cultural elements too conservative and patriarchal for a woman redefining herself as a feminist. She eventually earned more than one master's degree.

Shortly after landing in Vegas, she began working as a waitress and met my father, Richard, or "Richie." He was always well-dressed, usually in a freshly pressed three-piece suit, with his jet-black hair slicked straight back and wearing expensive, newly shined, black dress shoes on his feet. My mom was drawn to his deliberate confidence and charm. In her mid-twenties, her round Scandinavian features and bright blonde hair made her an attractive young woman. They came from two completely different worlds. My dad was born and raised in Revere Beach, Massachusetts, a coastal suburb on the outskirts of Boston. He exuded the accent and attitude typical of an East Coaster. After returning from the Vietnam War, he moved to Las Vegas and became the maître d for the Riviera, reporting directly to Frank "Lefty" Rosenthal, a Chicago gangster who paired up with Anthony "The Ant" Spilotro to oversee operations for mafia bosses in the Midwest. Rosenthal and Spilotro were played by Robert DeNiro and Joe Pesci in Martin Scorsese's acclaimed, "Casino."

I was already growing in my mother's womb when she and Dad were married in the winter of 1979. My dad had two daughters already, but both remained in the custody of his ex-wife until they were old enough to choose to come live in our family's middling, two-story home located on the edge of town across from Prosperity Park in what was then a smaller and less populated version of Las Vegas. Tall palm trees and oleanders bounded our swimming pool and jacuzzi deck where my dad spent hours lounging and sun tanning, a few feet away from the in-ground pool where his kids swam and played with rafts and giant beach balls.

The girls spent weekends with us until they decided to move in permanently when they were older. Perhaps they yearned for direction and stability from my mom, who may have left the Church but never wavered from the set of values my grandparents instilled in her. She was an excellent female role model to them and a stark contrast from Inez - Stephanie and Lisa's alcoholic, abusive mother. Inez suffered from untreated alcoholism which unfortunately fueled and instigated mayhem for my father and his growing family in the early years of my parents' marriage.

Alcoholism was the cause of numerous spoiled holidays and birthdays for all five of us kids, which included my younger brothers Nick and Tony, born two and seven years after me, respectively. The situation was especially bad for Stephanie and Lisa though, torn between abandoning their mother and protecting themselves from neglect and the perverted appetites of the dangerous men Inez dated. Lisa later described one of those men, named Armand, as creepy and predatory. He would expose himself to them through his robe when they were little girls. Years later, this sicko ended up on America's Most Wanted for raping someone's child. The emotional discord happening all around me was so palpable that I could detect it even at five years old. I felt so bad for my big sisters. We were all very close growing up.

My dad was becoming a very popular chef in Vegas during the 80's, and his extroverted characteristics played to his advantage in making social connections. They called him "Richie Boston" when he became an apprentice for the infamous Joe Pignatello, owner of the Villa D' Este, and Frank Sinatra's personal chef. My dad's reputation for cooking authentic Italian food expanded, and eventually he opened his own Italian deli. Here was my dad, cooking for celebrities and several high ranking and prominent mafia figures depicted in movies, and then he started a family business that was basically a hangout for violent hit men, judges, and racketeers.

Dad had lots of sociopathic friends back then, and there was always chaos around him. He and his wise guy pals, including his closest friend, Richie Perry, allegedly hired the starting line-up for the winning 1990 NCAA Running Rebels to be hosts at his deli-turned-restaurant. To this day, many believe this is the reason why Jerry Tarkanian has still not been inducted into the NCAA Hall of Fame, despite those championships. But that's a whole other book to be written. One thing is for sure, though. It was the beginning of the end for his family business. In the end, my dad had to testify in front of a grand jury.

"You never rat on your friends, Christopher, capisce?"

He was ready to go to prison for his friends if he had to. Oscar Goodman, a former Las Vegas mayor and legendary criminal defense attorney, made sure that didn't happen, though. He was another close friend of father and a frequent diner at Richie's Room, which was the name of Dad's restaurant.

Located on the corner of Spring Mountain and Rainbow in the 80's and early 90's, his restaurant was one of the few places in town where people with a taste for authentic Italian cuisine came to eat good food paired with fine Italian wines. What began as a small Italian deli eventually grew into a dinner destination frequented by some of the most famous and most dangerous connected families in Las Vegas. But my father is not a criminal nor a sociopath. Those types just really liked his food, and I think he really liked being around other Italians as nuts as he was. In fact, "Richie Boston" eventually became known as "Crazy Richie" in the Sicilian community.

Dad had a bad temper back then, but he was not an abusive father. He never hit his children or his wife, but when he got mad at someone, it was scary as hell to behold. I feared him, but I was also very proud that my dad didn't back down to anyone for anything. He didn't start fights with people, but God help the drunk man stupid enough to challenge him. To this day, he does not like to talk about his experiences in Vietnam. Only a few times was he willing to give details about the acts of violence that occurred all around him, and the near-death experiences that left even the most fearless men shell-shocked for life. Challenging a Vietnam veteran in a fight means you have challenged a man whose mind is conditioned to believe fighting equals "kill or be killed", so you better hope someone breaks up that fight fast if you find yourself on the losing end of it.

Drinking wine is traditional in Italian culture and on my father's side of the family, it was normal for the adults to get a little tipsy during any celebration. There was always something to celebrate, but my dad was a binge drinker, a symptom of his undiagnosed PTSD. When a person is drunk, there is always the possibility of verbal abuse. A few times, my dad was so plastered that the abhorrent things he said to my mother made me hate him, even if only temporarily. He was always very remorseful afterwards. But the damage inflicted on the victims of someone who is belligerently intoxicated can last a long time. My dad has a unique talent for using the F-word as a noun, verb, and adjective all in a single sentence. As a grown man now, I think it's hilarious when my dad swears in his Boston accent which, even after 50 years removed from his hometown, has stubbornly remained intact.

As a child, I felt frightened and unsafe when my dad lost his temper and began to viciously swear at an adversary or about opposition in his life, impulsively using profanity at high volumes. His destructive, drunken rampages at home were the exception to the norm though. I remember that happening only a handful of times. If my dad was going to party, he usually did so away from his wife and children, leaving my mother paralyzed with fear that something terrible would happen. Every time I saw my dad drunk, it was like the good man I loved and looked up to wasn't present, possessed by an overly animated, egocentric maniac with no filter.

I can't blame Crazy Richie for my addiction problems, though, because there are so many other contributing factors. His contribution is just the tip of the iceberg. It's a family disease that can be treated if a family is willing to participate in the subject's recovery. My dad has been in scary situations and seen things most people are fortunate enough to never experience. He always provided for his family and taught us to express love and affection for each other. Family is the most important part of his life. There is nothing I could do that would ever cause either of my parents to disown me, and thus they are following the example of the God I have come to believe in and have learned to lean on in that regard.

Chapter 6

True Friends & False Gods

My sister, Stephanie, is almost exactly three years older than me. We both have Gemini birthdays, which are only two days apart. As teenagers, we were partners in crime. Together, we methodically planned ways to get high and sneak out at night, eluding our parents from our shenanigans. When I was 15 years old, she persuaded me to grow my hair long and learn to play the guitar, with a promise that doing so would bring me popularity and play to my advantage in the high school dating circuit. My mom and dad hated this look so much they bought me a brand new electric guitar and amplifier in exchange for cutting my hair. I just grew it right back anyway – much longer the second time.

Some parents would probably say, "They should have just made him cut it." But this is the same dangerously oblivious mindset parents have when they find out their kid is using drugs and alcohol. The early reaction is almost always to exert control over their loved one, eventually shaming them when that strategy invariably fails.

My parents thankfully let their children be expressive and creative. I am not suggesting it's prudent to welcome little Johnny with a wink and smile if he shows up to dinner wearing a swastika on his face. However, I do think this would be a great opportunity to introspectively assess what factors at home have led the kid to become a neo-Nazi with violent ambitions. Most parents have too much pride to admit they could possibly have anything to do with the development of bad behaviors. Thus, in addiction, they are part of the problem until humility sets them free. It is a *family* disease.

Steph and I began to smoke a lot of weed and use LSD regularly. I attended Durango High School which had just been erected on the southwestern border of Vegas where Rainbow Boulevard ended back in 1994. Beyond was nothing but desert terrain with hidden caves and sunken pits exploited by teenagers who wanted to get wasted and party away from the watchful eye of Las Vegas Metro Police patrol cars. My sister remained at Bonanza High School because they gave her graduating class a zoning exception, maybe because changing schools would confuse the varsity football players. It was the 90's in Las Vegas, and the jocks were just as stoned as the rest of us.

Regardless of the difference in high school allegiance, we were part of the same social circle, consisting mostly of kids in local bands and troublemakers who were kicked out of Vegas schools on a regular basis for using drugs or fighting. My sister and her girlfriends were all very attractive girls, so when my buddies and I showed up at high school parties in the back seats of their cars, we were promptly met with welcoming fist bumps by the older guys who were much bigger than us. Like me, most of my friends were Kurt Cobain copies--our parted hair fell over our faces, ending at our chins. I wore baggy jeans, cut off at the bottom, and below a T-shirt with my favorite band's logo printed on the front. We skateboarded, did drugs, formed our own band, and chased girls. To us teenagers, life was that simple.

My drummer was a guy named Justin G, who, after 25 years of friendship, is like a brother to me. His ADHD was so frenzied that people either thought he was hilarious or wanted to murder him within 15 minutes of meeting him. I have seen him punched in the face more times than I can count. He spawned from two hippie parents who must have taught him that instead of hitting people back, he should say, "What the hell, bro?" because that was always his reaction, unless it was a girl that punched him. That happened sometimes too. He and I are the only two remaining members of our band who found Recovery before prison or death.

Justin's passion was to test the patience of authority figures and expose hypocrisy wherever possible. I loved this about him. In seventh grade, he was sent home by the dean for dying his hair purple. The next day, he came back to school with his hair dyed back to its original blonde color, brazenly wearing a dress with flowers on it, his blue eyes decorated with mascara, and red lipstick slathered around his mockingly clown-like smile. Justin is not transgender or even gay, for that matter. He just wanted to piss the dean off so she would unwittingly incite a debate among parents. It worked and was controversial enough that, in the end, she probably regretted picking on Justin for his hair color. When he set his mind to something, there was no mischief he could not achieve.

Justin once jumped on stage in the middle of a Hole concert and hugged the lead singer, Courtney Love. He was swiftly thrown out of the concert, handcuffed by the Hard Rock security team, and searched for drugs. Lucky for him, I had bought the weed that day, and had safely hidden it beneath the sole of my left Vans shoe. After somehow convincing them to let him walk out of the venue's front doors, protected by two large men in suits with earpieces, what he did next seemed impossible. I knew Justin and was dreading the blowback from what I sensed he was about to do.

"Don't, Justin," I said with a halfhearted smile. He looked like a pit bull fixated on a feline target, held back only by a leash.

The second they let him go, he darted back into The Joint, gliding through the arms of security with the doggedness of an NFL running back. The crowd protected him and eventually lifted him up to a crowd surf. At his request, they threw my cartoon-like friend back on the stage where he was reunited with the now furious Courtney Love. The second hug made her forget the words she was singing as she screamed, "You little 'F'n creep!" through the microphone in the middle of the song, *Doll Parts*. Justin proudly faced the crowd and threw his arms up in the air, satisfied he had made a fool of the Hard Rock security team, and frazzled the widow of the late lead singer for the band, Nirvana, who many people, including Justin, believed instigated Kurt Cobain's suicide in 1994 by relentlessly shaming him for using heroin. Thousands of spectators responded approvingly. Justin raised thundering laughter and applause before the police tackled him and threw him off the stage like a rag doll.

The late Scott Wieland of Stone Temple Pilots wrote a song, presumably about Courtney Love and Kurt Cobain, called, *Too Cool Queenie*. In the second verse he sings:

"There was this boy who played in a rock and band, and he wasn't half bad at saving the world. She said he could do no right, so he took his life, this story is true."

Weiland also struggled with heroin addiction and died from an overdose in 2012 after several failed attempts at rehabilitation. Linkin Park's Chester Bennington who, before success in his own band, had dreamed of one day becoming the singer for Stone Temple Pilots, and succeeded in making that dream come true when the band chose him to fill the big shoes of the iconic STP front man. Not long after, much like Kurt Cobain, Bennington died in an addiction-related suicide, a few months after the release of the highly praised final Linkin Park album, *One More Light*. He was actively involved in charities that supported the Recovery community. It's a tragedy this disease got the best of him.

These fallen rock stars all had one thing in common: shame. They had not addressed the sources of shame fueling their relentless desire to use. It may have stemmed from an event or events that occurred many years before their untimely deaths, or perhaps it was just the indignity of a recent relapse ending a long stretch of continued sobriety. Having a lot of money and fame and being a drug addict is a bad combination. For me, amassing wealth and esteem was the beginning of my undoing, and the start of my addiction to the most dangerous kinds of drugs.

Through Justin, I met Travis. He towered over both of us and something about his gummed smile and grumbling chuckle always made me laugh. He's the best lead guitar player I have ever known, and we riffed together with effortless grace, always knowing which pattern and progression the other would choose before it happened. Neither Justin or Travis graduated from high school or went to college, but they were both exponentially more intelligent than a lot of my friends who did.

All three of us came from homes where emotional dishonesty and familial discord was common, but for Travis, it was the norm. His dad was an abusive alcoholic who mistreated his mother, depending on her to provide while he sat home and got loaded with Travis and his friends. He was the "cool dad" when we were teenagers, but teens eventually don't respect the cool dad, because a man who refuses to grow up isn't worthy of respect. The drums were set up in Travis's room, and his father hovered around us drinking and smoking pot, gallingly offering his useless input to our developing songs. It always annoyed me when drunk people suddenly thought they were qualified to produce music. You would think a man who raised a musical prodigy would be proud of him, but Travis's dad was jealous and cruel. He was constantly tearing him down and calling him names. It's no wonder Travis had little confidence in himself, despite how exceptionally talented he was.

A teenager without a solid family will create his own. Some kids end up joining gangs, while others like Travis, Justin, Clint, Ryan, Kelley, Marc, and myself chose each other to be our family, complete with a common set of values. Justin and Clint were both Christian, possessing a close relationship to God and a religious obedience. Travis and I scoffed at it until an opportunity to play in the church band under the direction of a former Elvis Presley music arranger presented itself. "It can't hurt, dude," Travis said with a shrug. "Let's just learn everything we can from him, strictly for musical gain. It's not like they're going to brainwash either of us." We learned about diminished chords, how to transpose keys, and impeccable timing.

The music experience turned out great, but there was one problem: the belief system. I was warming up to the possibility of a god, but there were unanswered questions that nagged at me. The pastor was always preaching about the homosexuals and unsaved non-Christians destined to burn in the tormenting flames of hell, but the gay people and members of different faiths in my life were all good, honest people. Who was he to judge and condemn them?

Travis and I must have been thinking the exact same thing during a sermon in the winter of 1997. As we picked up our instruments and walked off the stage, we shook our heads disapprovingly, appalled by the judgment and hatred coming from the obese pastor's sagging mouth. The always intense Pastor Dan was glaring at both of us as he superciliously continued preaching, appearing pleased that his words had driven away two druggies who tainted his chapel with sin. Neither of us ever set foot in that place again, and a seed of hatred for Christianity was planted in our young minds that day.

Chapter 7

My Career

At 18 years old, it's fair to say I was more focused and goal-oriented than the guys I grew up with, but only because I was more afraid than they were. I wasn't smarter. The precarious situations I saw my friends in terrified me, and ironically the fear, which was half the reason I used drugs and alcohol in the first place, motivated me to mask the unmanageable symptoms of drug addiction for many years. The possibility of a drug overdose never worried me. But being arrested or losing my job was something I did everything in my power to control and prevent for as long as possible.

When I was 15, my dad got me a job as a lifeguard at the Aladdin Hotel and Casino, working for a guy who owed him a few favors. It covered the auto insurance and gas for the blue 1972 V8 Dodge Dart I purchased my high school junior year. But a seasonal hotel pool job treating drunk tourists for heat exhaustion and stacking lounge chairs wasn't going to pay rent for an apartment if I wanted to leave the nest. I wanted to escape the contention at home during the year of my parents ensuing divorce. So I took matters into my own hands and, for the first time in my life, I found respectable employment without using my father's connections.

When I started working at Las Vegas Reservation Systems for $8.00 per hour, no one could have predicted it would progress into a flourishing career with Expedia.com. The business model was one of the most brilliant ideas the hospitality industry had ever seen. Tim Poster and Tom Breitling were negotiating small allocations of hotel rooms from all the biggest casinos. Employees subsequently sold these over the phone to deal-searching customers bound for Sin City. To understand how ingenious this was, here's a crash course in Revenue Management:

Hoteliers almost always have rooms which go unsold, so dumping them off to groups and other booking sources at discounted rates increases overall profits. Hotel rooms are a perishable good, thus selling them for anything more than it costs to clean them, change the linens, and keep the power on is a win for the Revenue Manager tasked to optimize the REVPAR, or "Revenue Per Available Room Night." The customer gets an exclusive deal and the source of the booking takes a cut. Everybody wins.

Just as this thriving business seemed to be at the pinnacle of its success, something arrived that would revolutionize our economy and alter the way people purchased travel forever: the internet. And we were poised as the pioneers of online travel.

The bustling energy in our office was an intoxicating experience, making me hungry to learn everything I could about technology and business. The brilliant men and women who were my early mentors weren't just teaching me the online travel business. They were inventing it. Tim and Tom took the company public, and even the employees at lower levels were given stock options, with the first few thousand dollars' worth vesting after about a year. Before the options could mature, Expedia.com, a Microsoft spinoff under the leadership of a visionary named Rich Barton (founder of Expedia, Zillow, Glassdoor), acquired Travelscape.com in an $81.1 million deal. My modest incentive package vested immediately and just like that, I had over $10,000 in my bank account. At 20 years old, it was largest sum of money I'd ever had at once.

With hundreds of people now crammed into two detached buildings off Durango and Sahara, it wasn't long before we outgrew our offices. The company relocated to a large three-story structure in a wealthy, rapidly growing township called Summerlin, situated next to the Red Rock Mountains on the western edge of the Las Vegas valley. Expedia's new Las Vegas hub was bedecked with swanky office fixtures and a grandstanding architectural build which gave me the feeling I worked inside a government building with prodigious relevance where important people assembled every day to change the world. The top-floor executive offices on the northern wing boasted majestic views of the Las Vegas Strip, spanning from north to south and dividing the eastern and western sides of the city.

Once I realized that drinking was a socially acceptable practice within the professional community, I gave up smoking weed and replaced its dreamlike high with the soothing repose induced by overindulgent alcohol consumption. It provided a euphoric self-assurance which relaxed me and loosened my inhibitions, enabling me to confidently and intelligently converse with erudite colleagues I otherwise saw as better than me. Many of them were endowed with graduate degrees from Ivy League schools like Cornell and Georgetown, and I was an ordinary college drop-out, desperate to fit in with the most intimidating and brightest minds in our industry. The approval of my peers was important to me because I had no idea who I was. They knew me better than I knew myself, and their believing in my potential to cultivate a prosperous career was all the encouragement I needed to keep paying attention and take the advice given to me. I soaked up information like a sponge does water because I wanted to become a Market Manager, flown around the country and booked into luxury hotels on the company's dime like them. As a traveling businessman with a big salary and a respected title, I'd finally assume an identity suitable to my growing ego. I thought this would make me happy and fill the swelling void within my soul.

My sister, Stephanie, and her boyfriend moved in with me during the summer of 2001 to help me fulfill the terms of an apartment lease I had signed with my ex-girlfriend. She was my first love, and we had broken up on bad terms. Jodi was tall and slender, towering over me if she wore heels, standing eye-to-eye when barefoot. We lived together for a year of what seemed like endless dysfunction and emotional dissonance. She had grown up without a father and was taught that men can't be trusted because they will leave her when she needs them most. She and I were utterly co-dependent on one another, and our relationship was built on dueling insecurity and lustful obsessions, dooming it from the start.

Toxic relationships are one of the biggest triggers for me to turn to drugs and alcohol, second only to being trapped in my mind with the ghostly memories of a former lover after one has ended. I was glad to have the company of my big sister and her long-term boyfriend there to remind me that life goes on, even with a broken heart.

On the morning of September 11th, I was with my sister and her boyfriend in the living room area of our apartment before getting ready for work and departing to our different jobs. Steph had recently graduated from UNLV and was teaching high school math. I was still laser-focused on working toward the Market Manager position at Expedia.com. I woke up that morning drawn to the smell of freshly brewed coffee and made my way down the narrow hallway, offering a "good morning guys" with the little enthusiasm I could muster at 6:00 a.m.

Their eyes were fixated on an ABC news broadcast which showed live footage of the first World Trade Center tower in flames. "A plane crashed into a huge building in New York, bud. This won't be good for your industry, that's for sure," my sister said with cynicism. I trembled thinking about the people who had just lost their lives and the others still trapped in the building, some impossibly deciding to jump to their deaths instead of being burned alive. Just as the reporter noted that the rescue effort hadn't reached the top floors yet, the three of us watched in horrifying real-time as the second plane hit. Our jaws dropped and my sister began to cry. I knew right away what had happened. "Our country is under attack, Steph. We are probably going to have to go to war," I said, shaken with conflicting emotions of sadness, fear, and anger.

There was a palpable unease at the Expedia offices over the next few weeks as other companies began to announce massive layoffs. The airlines and hotel companies were hit the hardest. This obviously concerned everyone who made a living in travel. I rarely spoke up or shared my thoughts in the weekly business review meetings in which the Market Managers were required to present. I was invited there as part of a secret grooming process, but at the time, I had no idea why I was there. The senior management team really liked my energy, but I had yet to prove myself as anything more than a team mascot that made them laugh, and efficiently completed menial tasks.

Many of the Market Managers were complaining about how the hotel rates had gone down so much that meeting their revenue goals would now be next to impossible. "Just sell more rooms," I piped up. I couldn't believe I had interrupted the Market Manager for Phoenix with a four-worded sentence that came out sounding like a nine-year-old had said it. Still, it caught the curiosity of Jim, our division's Senior Vice President for lodging.

"Chris, elaborate on that," he said with an unconvincing attempt to look serious. This was my moment to shine.

"Well, she said the average rate in her market has dropped from $150 to $110. If she can persuade the expensive hotels to offer exclusive deals and agree to higher margins in exchange for more exposure, the average rate will go back up, with more rooms sold. Sell more rooms at the expensive hotels by making them less expensive. They will agree to it because they are desperate. Your customers are only booking your cheapest hotels. That's why the average rate is down. Shift your business away from them to the four-star hotels by pushing for a more appealing price point."

I was smarter than I thought, and had finally earned the respect of everyone in my department. I was promoted within a month and made the Market Manager for Minneapolis, St. Louis, and Kansas City.

Chapter 8
The Big Red Flag

My friends and family were perplexed by the sudden changes in my lifestyle as sweeping financial success followed my big promotion. My dad would say something funny when he asked about it like, "Buddy, are you in the (explicit) CIA or something? It's either that or you're a (explicit) hit man for the mob."

At barely 21 years old, I was making more money than everyone in my family, including both of my recently divorced parents. I purchased a new car and was renting an upmarket, luxuriously furnished Summerlin apartment with expensive appliances and a $2000 pillow-top mattress in the master bedroom. If I wanted something, I bought it, recklessly believing I could indulge in the pleasures of the world with infinite impunity.

Using cocaine was an expensive habit, which usually limited it to a weekend indulgence that rounded off a night of heavy drinking. I tried to buy only stuff that was high in purity, because lower quality "Blow" caused my nose to run excessively, leaving me congested with a self-induced cold the next morning. Some drug dealers cut their product before distributing it to maximize profit, often with baby laxatives or cold medicines that were never intended to go up a person's nose.

The effects of cocaine hit me quickly, energizing me and inducing synthetic feelings of joy. It made socializing more fun and inspired engaging conversations within the group. "This is safe; I'm only doing it because it boosts my confidence," I'd mentally reassure myself, as I purposefully divided the white powdery substance into straight, even lines before swiftly sticking the straw into my nostril. "All systems go and ready for take-off now," I'd think, as if my mind was a rocket I was preparing to launch into outer space.

There wasn't any discomfort as it passed through my nose into the tiny blood vessels inside my septum, dispersing into my bloodstream and circulating into my brain's reward center to arouse pleasurable feelings. After a few minutes, the excess drained into the back of my throat, briefly stirring a bitter taste in my mouth and numbing my teeth, reminding me of the tingly onset I'd feel after my dentist injected lidocaine into my gums prior to drilling into a decaying tooth.

It didn't take me long to retain a drug dealer who was consistent and readily available, usually answering my call by the third ring when I dialed on a Friday or Saturday night. Stevo was a bartender at a hole-in-the-wall bar called the Lighthouse where my friends and I frequently hung out for happy hour and at night on the weekends. Usually, a bartender can comp your tab if you're willing to put your money into the bar's built-in slot machines that are standard in most Las Vegas drinking establishments. Every time I fell for this trick, it cost me ten times what I would have paid for the price of four beers.

Gambling is one of the most destructive addictions I've ever witnessed, and I have seen its tempestuous lure consume close friends and family members. Sitting on a bar stool in a cloud of my own cigarette smoke, I began to think of something my father mentioned to me years before regarding gambling. "Buddy, when these kids come into my bar and hit a Royal Flush, I always shake my head because they are hooked for life," he said with accented East Coaster absolution. Winning money floods the brain with dopamine, much like the rush cocaine or other powerful drugs produce.

Stevo stood across from me with a surprised look. "You're not playing tonight, Buddy?" he asked in a fading Brooklyn accent. But without waiting for my answer, he nodded admiringly, his body language saying, "Good idea, kid."

Stevo had a white beard and white hair, reminding me of a degenerate alcoholic Santa

Clause actor, perhaps resembling a character I had seen in an old Christmas movie as a child.

"Nah, I am good, Stevo. Just give me the tab today, pal," I said, signing my name at the bottom of the receipt he placed before me.

"Your last name is Foresta?" Stevo inquired after reading the name printed on my debit card. "I know your dad, Richie. You look just like him." He was younger than my father and had worked with him at the Riviera "in the good old days" of Vegas.

Stevo was a heavy cocaine user throughout most of his life, and at some point, he began to sell it to subsidize the cost of his own habit.

When my dad found out about this, he went ballistic and as usual overreacted, threatening to blow up the Lighthouse while Stevo was inside if he didn't stop selling me drugs. "Your dad is just as crazy as ever. Don't let him find out I'm still selling you this shit," he said with a friendly smile, but still willingly accepting my money in exchange for cocaine despite the threats my dad had made.

Stevo was about sixty-five years old at the time, with a pacemaker surgically implanted inside of his chest following a serious heart attack, likely caused by relentless drug abuse. A few years after I met him, he overdosed, dying in the ambulance before he could reach the hospital. At his funeral, the only people in attendance were a few has-been mobsters who had aged past their primes, with sunken faces weathered by years of violence and debauchery. When I told my dad about Stevo's passing, all he could say was, "Poor kid, God rest his soul. Christopher, you've never seen a more handsome SOB than Stevo in his younger years. He had the world by the balls. What a shame."

Stevo was fueling my growing cocaine habit, but he also looked out for me and kept me safe from more nefarious drug dealers. Should he have listened to my dad and stopped getting me that stuff? Perhaps, but at least Stevo wasn't going to sell me a bag of dried bleach or something.

For me, the many problems of regularly using cocaine started with the short time frame in which the euphoric feelings faded away, replaced with crushing misery as the effects faded in" withdrawal were some sinus congestions, leading to a restless night of sleep. But psychologically, it was a punishing few hours of desolation and despair, persisting until my dopamine receptors replenished themselves and restored the delicate chemical balance in my brain so feelings of natural joy were possible again.

I was spending thousands of dollars a month feeding this weekend habit. It felt worth it to me to have the kind of confidence and sense of positive outlook I lacked naturally, if even for a few hours. Still, the following day that misery that would set in and it brought me to my knees. I vowed to never again put myself through this nightmare. Then, just as it always had, opportunity sprang through my door without ever knocking. My boss had been calling my phone all morning on a summer morning in 2003 when I called in sick due to the massive amount of drinking and using drugs I had done.

Her name is Nan. She had Avery's calm and quiet disposition. She was kind, but direct and unafraid to hurt someone's feelings if she believed it would help them.

"Hello?" I answered. I was trying to make it sound like I had a very bad cold. It would have sounded authentic as my nose was completely stuffed up with whatever the cocaine drug lords had put in it to cut it.

"Hi Chris, it's Nan. I guess you're not feeling too good today huh, bud?" Her tone was genuine and I was relieved to hear no discernable note of disappointment in her voice.

The next words she spoke not only lifted my spirts, but they created enough of a dopamine production to jolt my lazy body up from the messy bed I laid sleeping in moments before.

"Pack your bags. You are moving to Chicago, and Chris, one thing," she said with an audible comedic sarcasm.

"Yes, Nan, what is it?" I asked, thinking she was going to chew me out for calling in.

"Make better friends in Chicago."

Chapter 9

The Disease that Followed Me Everywhere

The temporary, corporate apartment Expedia relocated me to in the fall of 2005 was on the 21st floor of a high-rise building in the Gold Coast neighborhood of Downtown Chicago. My short walk to work included crossing over one of 18 retractable bridges which channeled a colossal workforce over the Chicago River and into the financial district, commonly referred to as "The Loop."

How did I end up here? I was lying on my bed, staring into the majestic, big-city scenery visible even as heavy rain was crashing down onto my bedroom's weather-beaten window.

The elegantly furnished unit rented for $3,500 per month, but it was free to me for the first three months as part of a generous relocation package Expedia offered when I agreed to move earlier that year. I quickly acclimated to the teeming environment. The sounds of taxi cabs honking and trains blowing by me became less distracting over time and eventually, even quite comforting. The peripheral backdrop was a material jungle of tall buildings, with the Sears Tower and John Hancock buildings dominating the skyline, each more than 100 stories high. The sidewalks swarmed with people passing through pleasant smells of world-class fare coming from a seemingly infinite array of restaurants and food stands. I simultaneously felt big and small as one of the millions of people who resided in this eccentric city, established next to the milieu of Lake Michigan many years ago.

My successful performance in developing the Minneapolis business was the main reason I was presented this opportunity. The fact that five of the other Market Managers in Vegas were not willing to move worked to my advantage when I negotiated the terms with our Human Resources department. The move was not mandatory. Everyone based in the Vegas hub was given the option to be reassigned to a territory.

I wasn't married and didn't have any children then, and the only thing I left behind was access to my expansive network of drug dealers and a group of friends who were going nowhere in life. Realizing my expensive cocaine habit was getting dangerously out of control, I assumed this would be a good way to escape all the bad influences in my life. However, I have come to realize I never really find temptation—it finds me. It doesn't matter how far I move because evil doesn't accede to manmade borders.

There is darkness everywhere in the world, and it took me a very long time to realize it's up to me to turn the lights on when I find myself in dark places.

Throughout my life, many people have attempted to steer me in the right direction, willing to take me under their wing both professionally and philosophically. My friendship with Utpal Kaul began as work colleagues in Summerlin. When news broke about a satellite office opening in Chicago, I called and urged him to apply for the Director position. He was born to be a teacher, and I couldn't think of anyone I would rather report to daily. I needed a good friend to lean on since I was moving to Chicago alone.

Utpal is from India, having moved to America in 2001 to complete his master's degree at Cornell prior to joining Expedia in 2003. I found his thick Hindi accent to be waggishly fascinating, with his labiodental W/V words reversed, and the pronunciation of T, D, and N sounds pronounced with his tongue curled back.

I was about 23 years old when we met, and my understanding of his culture was limited to satire portrayals of Indian characters in comedy movies. We were introduced by our boss, Kari, a tenacious, detail-oriented Manager who led our region's team.

"Christopher, this is Utpal. He will be joining our team as the Market Manager for New Orleans," she said, incorrectly pronouncing his name Oot Paul, with the correct way being uh t Paul. To this day, she and I both still say it wrong out of habit. "It's very nice to meet you," Utpal said, as he shook my hand and nodded politely. "I bet his friends are terrorists," I thought to myself, so pathetically uneducated at that age that I didn't even know the difference between Hinduism and radical Islam.

We quickly became friends, spending afternoons playing pranks on each other and on the other members of our team. In the evening, we'd sometimes have drinks together, and I would have a ton of questions for him about the world, and him for me about the nuances of our strange American culture. At the time, he seemed to be an expert in everything but that.

The new office space in Chicago was on the 23rd floor of a high-rise building on Lasalle Boulevard. The view from my office was a lot like the one from my apartment - tall buildings and bad weather. Sometimes I would zone out and watch the wind blow the snow upwardly, almost making me feel like I was turned upside down.

Utpal's office was next to mine, and he often stormed in, tersely giving instructions to his growing team. Because we were a satellite office, we all felt the intense pressure to grow the business and make it a success. He pushed me harder than any manager ever had for that reason, but also because he couldn't stand to see me squander my potential.

When your best friend becomes your boss, it invariably changes the nature of your relationship. Even today, one of our favorite things to do is argue with each other. It doesn't matter what the topic is, or which position the other chooses to support. If there is a controversial subject, we both pick a side and debate it. The object of the game is to convince the other to yield.

"Dude, I won the debate," he said with a grin, having learned the word "dude" from me years prior.

"Utpal, you did not win the debate, dude. There is no way legalizing gay marriage is going to open the door for people to marry their dogs," I responded, annoyed and unsatisfied that his argument was sound enough to claim a victory.

This is an example of the things we would dispute when we weren't disagreeing about the best course of action to grow the Minneapolis market.

In Chicago, our impromptu bantering about politics, religion, and social issues could last for hours. When I entered his office, it was usually to seek guidance on something that had nothing to do with my job. What began as an unlikely friendship in Las Vegas became that of a mentor and student. The contrast of his Indian accent and extensive vocabulary made him sound even wiser. This is probably how the Karate Kid felt when taking direction from Mr. Miyagi.

Utpal is one of the smartest men I have ever known. He fed my young, fertile mind new information and ideas by challenging me with complex questions I would have otherwise never cared to ask. He figured out that if he pissed me off enough, I would research a subject until I knew enough to prove him wrong. This was his way of tempering my ADD, so I would push myself harder and become better. I believe that was always his brotherly intention.

We spent about ten years working alongside one another at Expedia. Reporting to Utpal gave me an unfair advantage in many ways. When he accepted the role in Chicago becoming my director, he also became keeper of my career and the person responsible for appraising my performance. He never gave me a raise or performance I did not earn, but toward the end, he knew that holding me accountable for my poor job performance would likely lead to my eventual termination. After my divorce, I began to use drugs and alcohol so forcefully that I was working from home, in bed, on my laptop.

Utpal is one of the most loyal people I have ever known. I eventually realized he was preventing me from facing catastrophic consequences on a regular basis. He did not understand completely what was happing to me. After all, there was a time when I was praised for my success as an underdog who had accomplished so much, despite never stepping foot in a university. One of the last conversations we had in his office was behind closed doors, about one month before he left the company.

"It has been a few years since your divorce, Chris. How are you doing, my friend?"

We hadn't sat in the same room for several months. In the final year that both of us were Expedia employees, I had relocated back to Las Vegas while Utpal moved to Bellevue, Washington where the company's headquarters are.

"I have accepted a new position within a new company, dude," he explained with a forced smile on his face.

It was not like Utpal to start a conversation on a topic this serious without first introducing some sort of ice breaker. Maybe a filthy joke, or an office prank, but today was different.

He continued, "You are like a little brother to me, and I have always looked after you. You will have a new manager and you must make some serious changes fast."

I didn't insult him by pretending I was confused and asking what he meant by that comment. I knew what he was referring to. When I returned to Vegas, I was reassigned the states of Arizona and New Mexico, within the larger Mountain Region which Utpal now oversaw. I loved Chicago, and the only reason I moved home was to avoid reporting to someone else.

He paused for a few seconds and then continued, "I may have done you a disservice as a friend and mentor by failing to hold you accountable. Something far beyond the impact your divorce could have had on you has impacted your performance, and more so, it has fundamentally changed you. I hardly recognize you."

I wish I would have fessed up that day. I was heavily addicted to pain killers and experimenting with heroin. I looked terrible, and it was visually obvious I wasn't eating healthy or sleeping much. My clothes were wrinkled and my hair and beard unkempt. I looked 10 years older than I was. Utpal would have gotten me into rehab before I lost my job.

"It's just depression, Utpal. I will see the doctor." This was a half-truth.

His concerned farewell to me was, "Your next manager will not rescue you the way I have. Take better care of yourself."

After leaving the office, I waved down a taxi to drive me to my hotel. Any time I visited our headquarters in Seattle, I stayed at the Hyatt Regency Bellevue. I always stayed in luxury hotels on business trips for Expedia. Aside from the fact that I was allowed to expense just about everything, the hotel portion was also comped by the hotel. They were happy to extend these invitations to Expedia Market Managers since I had the ability to fill empty rooms in a few hours for a hotel willing to provide an attractive deal. I was the person who sat behind a massive, well-oiled marketing machine deciding what deal millions of people would see that evening.

My accommodations were not just complimentary. When I checked in, my name was at the top of the VIP list. This, of course, had nothing to do with being Chris Foresta. I just happened to be the lucky son of a gun with the power to make others a ton of money. At twenty-five years old, I believed I was better than others and entitled to the privileged life I was living.

Upon exiting the taxi, I was greeted by a bellman who took my bags while another held the door into a large atrium appointed with lavish lighting. A line of people filed back from the front desk waiting to be checked in. I received disapproving looks from several of them as I walked straight to the front of the line. It wasn't obvious I was heading to the VIP check-in until I reached the counter. The clerk requested my driver's license. She made a copy, and then placed it into an envelope which also contained my electronic keycard.

"Your room is on the top floor, Mr. Foresta," the front desk attendant said with a friendly smile. "Please be sure to present your keycard to the security guard before entering the private access elevators, which are down the hall," she said, gesturing the direction I should go.

I wondered why there was even a button for the 24th floor because it was the only option. Just as I pressed it, someone yelled, "Hey man, hold that door, my dude!" The well-dressed black men with giant gold chains drooping from their necks walked straight past the security guard who simply nodded and waved them onto the platform. I looked up from my Blackberry and realized I was sharing an elevator with Usher. At the prime of his music career, he was scheduled to perform later that evening. I glanced at the group long enough to extend a friendly greeting but pretended to have no idea who he was.

When I got to my room, the first thing I did was a big line of cocaine and a shot of vodka. I gazed out the window and thought about what

Utpal had said earlier that day. I had never considered what might happen if I lost this high paying job. I did not have a college degree, and my achievements were the result of a little hard work and an enormous amount of luck.

Eventually, I did lose all of my worldly possessions. In their place, I was taught humility and the value of personal sacrifice. I went to hell and back, and in that process, a power greater than me decided it was time to trim and temper that overgrown, arrogant ego of mine.

PART 2

Chapter 10

Building Me Up Just to Burn it All Down

The 60 days I spent in-house at Renaissance Ranch in 2013 was a transformative period of personal discovery for me. My outlook on life had improved, and I was clean and sober for the first time in almost 20 years. There was not a single mind-altering substance to influence my thoughts or actions through the abysmal bondage that is dependency. My reward for enduring the therapy sessions for two straight months was the restoration of my agency. This was a small price to pay in hindsight.

Suddenly, there was very little supervision. In the first weeks following treatment, I was already questioning things about addiction and recovery I was taught not to question. The answer to this question is not what any addict new to recovery wants to hear. So many of us resist. Can we ever drink or use like others do now that we are clean and sober? After all, I know plenty of people who can moderate their alcohol consumption. The question is, can I? In other words, the idea that my tolerance could be reset so I could drink like a gentleman was almost as intoxicating as drinking was.

This train of thought is so dangerous and so destructive a road, for to this day, when it creeps up, I immediately distract myself with anything else because I know my ego wants to believe I can, even though I know it's a big fat ugly demonic lie.

This is probably one of the reasons people in Recovery never refer to themselves as cured. If the addictive nature of my brain was cured, then I would use and drink whenever I wanted with impunity. It's not cured. It's in remission. When this concept was first introduced to me, it sounded something like this, "If someone is obese, can they be cured? Of course not. They can diet and exercise and change their lifestyle, and the fat starts to disappear, but they have to continue with these new healthy habits. Otherwise, they will get fat again. So diet and exercise did not cure them from being fat, the lifelong commitment to changing did. My brain is different. I can't have a glass of red wine with my steak. I can't even have a sip. If I break a bone, someone else must hold on to my bottle of pain killers, and if I can get by without them, well, even better.

The 12 steps of Alcoholics Anonymous were introduced to me through Renaissance Ranch. There are other treatment models, but most of them include a long commitment to narcotic medications which felt counterintuitive to me. The only issue I had with working the 12 steps was all the "Higher Power" related step work which required me to rely on gods I did not believe in. However, once I was told I get to define this high power the way I want to, and that belief in a religion was not part of it, I became willing to exercise a small amount of faith. It paid off. I actually do believe in God now and am a member of a church. None of that was ever the intention, or even a prerequisite to succeeding in the program. There are plenty of atheists, much like I used to be, who still have found Recovery through the 12 steps. That's important to note.

At the time I went into treatment, I was about as anti-God as one can be, but in many ways, that was an asset which would fast-track me through some of the stages in my progression. Sometimes the shame associated with religion is one of the primary causes and conditions that addiction can flourish inside someone.

I did not in any way believe that a god was going to punish me if I failed at something. But many of my friends in recovery were convinced that was exactly why they were there - for punishment. I remember a conversation with a friend I will not name who had admitted that every time he masturbated, he wanted to use meth because the shame he felt was overwhelming and the drug would bring some relief.

"I'm pretty sure you just said that backwards," I responded.

I grinned and scratched at my head because I actually did assume that he had just misspoken. Meth is a stimulant and thus by nature an aphrodisiac which causes stronger sexual urges in most people. Many intentionally use it before sex.

"You mean after you got high on meth you would go whack-off, right, dude? Hey man, that's better than unsafe sex."

I wasn't being funny either. I came from an entirely different background. The point I'm getting at is, I did not grow up in a household that taught masturbation was something you should be ashamed of. My parents were happy as long as we didn't make grandkids a premature reality for them.

"Well, I masturbate because I have urges, then I use because it helps with the shame," said the brother who shall remain nameless. "God sees us when we masturbate, bro. Why do you think we are all being punished like this?"

I laughed so hard I spit out my drink, but it's actually quite sad that he believed God turned him into a drug addict for touching his own penis. These misguided beliefs are why people are afraid to accept all of the good that spiritual programs like AA and the 12 steps are capable of producing.

Religious shame was not a trigger for me, but I still had triggers. This disease is patient. It counts on me becoming over-confident that I have been cured. The number one trigger in my life, which has always lit the fuse to a relapse, is the negative emotion associated with relationship conflict.

I married Monica and adopted her son, Mason, in the winter of 2015. She is the love of my life, and Mason is my life. I would die for either of them in a New York second. She and I met in a Recovery meeting, and within months, we were creating enough chaos in each other that avoiding relapse was an unlikely proposition, especially because our busy lives as newlyweds had pushed Recovery meetings to the back burner. It was a beautiful disaster. Relapse was inevitable, but what no one saw coming was the length of time the relapse would last. I got high three months into our marriage, and it went on for four more years. What follows is my account of descending into the darkest places I never thought I would see.

Being in a relationship with another addict is definitely not a suggestion you will hear very often, but there are advantages, just as there are disadvantages. Monica and I know each other more intimately than most unions ever will. We were told that once we had used together, it would not be possible for us to remain married.

We took that as a challenge! But that story is for another time.

Chapter 11

The Land of the Lost and Forgotten

My first night alone on the streets of downtown Salt Lake City was in the winter of 2017. It was cold enough that sleeping outside was not an option. The homeless shelter was a hub for drug sales, so I loitered on the streets that surrounded it. I had hit rock bottom again, concerned only with having easy access to heroin and a warm place to sleep at night. The shelter is a two-story structure situated next to the Rio Grande station, in an area commonly referred to as "The Block" by addicts and drug dealers. There are male and female entrances on opposite sides of the building which sits between 400 West and 500 West on the corner of 200 South.

I was familiar with this location, having frequented the area many times over the years to buy drugs. Of course, I previously never had a reason to stay more than 10 minutes, having traveled there in a car to purchase drugs. As I got off the train and started making my way to the shelter, I paused for a moment and considered the state of my life. I was a failure in every way possible, including abandoning my wife and son who were fortunately safe at my in-laws without a father and husband to provide for them.

For my whole life, people had told me how talented and intelligent I was, how much potential I had. So, what the hell happened? How had I become homeless? The shame set in, and as I pondered these questions, a dark cloud of regret and hopelessness enveloped me.

"I need to get high. I can't stand these feelings!" I thought to myself as I purposefully made my way toward the only thing I knew would relieve the anguished pattern of thinking afflicting me. I was drawing dangerously closer to flirting with suicidal ideations every day.

The presence of evil was everywhere, an invisible parasite feeding off human suffering and the senseless acts of violence the addicted and mentally ill population commit on each other. As I looked up at others who passed me, I was met with mostly brief glances, looks of dread, and worry. They were as uninterested in my plight as I was in theirs. Others glared at me with a predatory, psychotic, wolf-like stare, fixating on me for many seconds as if they were deciding whether to make me their next target of prey. I quickly realized I needed to be prepared to protect myself against people with nothing to lose, some willing to rob me for a single cigarette, if that was the only obtainable item available to plunder. Wolves target weak prey that seem easy to defeat, so I changed my rhythm and started to exude a wild confidence. I remembered something my dad told me as a child being picked on by a bigger kid at school. "Christopher, there is nothing deadlier and scarier than a crazy man. You show that kid, with your eyes, that you are ready to kill him if you have to, and he ain't going to want nothing to do with you." Alone in a concrete jungle with danger lurking around every corner, I took his advice, adapting to my surroundings as a lone wolf.

As I walked alone through the dark alleyways of Salt Lake City, I had only one goal. I needed to find the one thing that would pacify the immense flood of feelings I was powerless to manage myself. I was in the land of the wayward and forgotten. On every corner of every street were people like me who, long ago, were innocent children with dreams of prosperity and success. I never made the decision to invite drug addiction into my life, but like many of the destitute souls who occupied the streets in the malodorous slums where I now resided, my own choices had led me to this dark and lonely place.

Creatures of the night were around every corner, under a dark spell which compelled them to seek a means to an end that would fulfill their selfish, misguided desires. Crack cocaine, heroin, spice, and methamphetamine are the instruments of evil Satan uses in his attempt to reign over the "cracking" streets to the west of downtown Salt

Lake City. Urban lawlessness shadowed the luminous Salt Lake City LDS temple's glow.

Every homeless drug addict is a con. Some group up like a pack of wolves, using strength in numbers to allow them to circle in on vulnerable prey. I had never been homeless before, and I was now relying on my instincts to survive in this penniless new world. Many times, I put myself in dangerous situations that could have violently ended my life.

The sounds of random cries and loud shrieks that rang through the night were an unsettling soundtrack. Anyone sober enough to realize the insanity of this existence would be terrified. I did not have time to be frightened by people, places or things. My sole fear was the impending dope sickness which would arrive by morning if I let the clock run out, leaving me too sick to function and too frail to move.

I carried a backpack with everything I owned neatly packed inside--a change of clothes, sundries, a tablet, and some cigarettes and a lighter. The only other thing I needed to feel safe was a few balloons of heroin. As I traveled on a road that led to nowhere, this was the insane thinking that piloted every decision I would make that night.

When attempting to make a drug deal with strangers, I quickly learned how to properly signal my intent. First, I made eye contact, followed by an upward nod of the head. This meant you either had something or wanted something. The safest bet was to approach a person of Honduran descent. For a long time, this ethnic group dominated the heroin and crack business of Salt Lake City. But in 2016, the local government created an initiative called Operation Rio Grande to disrupt the organization by the force of added police. This was effective in pushing the Honduran gangs out and to this day, very few of them remain. However, all this did was give other groups a chance to prosper through illegal trade. The only difference now is that a buyer is taking a risk that they will be sold something fake, or perhaps just be robbed outright.

Two men were approaching on the horizon, dragging towards me with a gangster-lean swagger. Earlier, I had stopped at a pawn shop to trade a cheap tablet for fourteen dollars - just a dollar short of the price tag on a heroin balloon, certainly enough to complete the transaction I was urgently pursuing if I was direct.

The first was a heavy-set black man with an unkempt beard wearing a white Nike T-shirt and baggy jeans which sagged down, revealing his boxer shorts. His shirt generously covered the entirety of his wide body, hanging low enough to appear like a modest church gown. He was probably in his twenties. I met his gaze and offered a nod as I spoke, "What up, man, you got black?"

I didn't hesitate to state my purpose. In an exchange like this, there is always a mutual concern that someone is a police officer. But the burden rests mostly on the seller. Cops have little interest in trapping a drug addict. They want to catch the men and women distributing it.

I found it hilarious when they asked me that question. Anyone can look like an undercover cop, but I am the furthest thing from it. Some drug dealers believe that if they ask you this question and you are a police officer, the law states you must answer honestly. This is not true, but I answered the question before it could be asked anyway. "I am not a cop."

He turned his head both ways, scanning the area for law enforcement. This kind of nervous behavior made me feel confident I wasn't talking to a scam artist. If his drugs were fake, arrest wouldn't be on his mind. Nevertheless, it's not uncommon to be sold packed dirt or a pebble wrapped in a balloon.

I still wasn't sure of this guy's intent, but usually when it's a rip-off attempt, these gestures are overly dramatic. His fear of arrest was palpable enough to earn my trust. I was confident he was about to commit a felony by selling me drugs.

"What you need, fool?" He was squinting his eyes the way a person would when angry as he asked that question.

"Just one dog," I answered nervously, as the adrenaline began to pour through me. I performed my own scan of the area, trusting my own line of sight better than that of a stranger to ensure this was a safe place to commit a crime of my own.

"Give me your money."

Out of context, that line might have sounded more like the start of a mugging then a drug deal, but I had done this enough to understand his intent. Still, I had been robbed plenty of times, and I knew better than to hand over my net worth without some sort of assurance this would end in a fair trade.

"I need to see it first, man, you know how it is, right?" I was negotiating now and trying to persuade a potentially dangerous criminal to meet me halfway. He performed one last scan and looked back at me with a friendlier expression than the first.

"Yeah, man, it's tough with the Hondo gone, huh? Here, dawg, it's even opened. You can smell it."

He was much larger than me. Giving me possession before receiving my payment probably didn't concern him in the least bit. There was no one watching. If he wanted to, he would have already knocked me out and taken everything I owned.

Most heroin is a black tar, but sometimes it comes in a powdery brown form. The latter is usually more potent and requires the user to introduce moisture by breathing warm air on it so it can be smoked on foil. This was the only way I ever consumed it. I have a fear of needles, which is a good thing for a heroin addict. It smells like vinegar, and after time, the distinctive odor is unmistakable. His product was legit.

Realizing I was satisfied, he held out his hand, motioning for me to pay him without words.

"I am a dollar short, man," I said to him.

He accepted it anyway, saying nothing back, and just like that, he and his buddy disappeared back into the dark, cold night.

When I was homeless, I never had a specific destination once in the possession of heroin and the paraphernalia required to consume it. Heroin must be smoked indoors unless the air is perfectly still; otherwise, the wind blowing out your flame is the least of your troubles. Inhaling heroin into the lungs is done differently than most other illegal drugs, using an apparatus that channels the smoke directly into the lungs right from the source of the flame. Heroin is placed on foil and a flame ignites the smoke from beneath it. One must chase the smoke with a straw to breathe it into the lungs.

At 2:00 a.m., I didn't have the option of exploiting a fast-food bathroom stall. On a windy January evening, the homeless shelter would now be my best bet.

The Roadhouse is a massive two-story building on the corner of Rio Grande and 200 South. The walls were made of cinder block painted a dreadful yellow color. Beautification isn't an option for homeless shelters, and it felt more like I was entering a county jail than a refuge. I passed a line of men in hooded coats, smoking cigarettes. They looked me up and down as they leaned against the structure where I ascended from a wheelchair ramp. After entering through the doors of the pavilion, I was met by a Middle Eastern man sitting at a desk. He was watching a soccer game on his phone. The announcers were speaking a language I couldn't place, perhaps Arabic or Farsi. He looked up at me and asked me for my first and last name in broken English.

"Thank you, sir," he answered after I told him. "Please enter through the metal detectors and leave your bags to be searched. Are you carrying any weapons or drugs?" He asked the questions as if on autopilot, likely having gone through this script hundreds of times already that evening.

I had anticipated the search and made sure my balloon was in my mouth. In a worst-case scenario, I could swallow it to avoid arrest. It comes out the same way it goes in, which is why it is packaged that way. After lazily glancing into my bag, he assigned me a room and bed number and turned his attention back to his sports broadcast. I realized a person could easily enter this place with a lethal weapon. It made me nervous. "This is where I am sleeping tonight," I thought to myself.

The halls were lined with stacked garbage bags full of clothes. Suddenly, chaos began to ensue. I could hear the commotion coming from down the hall and began to realize what was going on.

"Make way for the EMT's!" a man with a walkie-talkie in his hand shouted.

I backed up to the wall as a group of paramedics rushed by me pushing a badly beaten man on a stretcher. He appeared to need life support. The other residents watched in horror, and I could sense they felt the same fear as me.

A bald man with tattoos on his face, a long goatee, and sporting a black eye stood next to me. He had followed the medics to this point, so I assumed he would have more information than me. I asked, "Dude, what the heck happened to that guy?"

His head hung down and he appeared to be unhappy. "They jumped him and took his Clear, bro. He had like two hundred dollars' worth. That is my dog. I'm going to get them back."

His sorrow turned to rage as he answered and I thought, I'm glad I'm not part of "them." He was clearly a brawler.

Now several police were approaching, scuffling three handcuffed men through the corridor who were angry and shouting expletives as they moved through the halls. Once they reached the point where we stood, one of the handcuffed fellows darted towards us and spit in the tattooed man's face, then into mine.

As bad as the homeless shelter seemed at the time, it was a refuge from the cold, snowy winter nights. The homeless spend a lot more time outdoors then one might expect. Today, when I see a man or a woman begging for change on the corner of a street in the city, I feel empathy and compassion that I would not have been susceptible to many years ago.

I have lived in high places, low places, and everything in between. The notion of "that would never happen to me" no longer exists in my thought process. If there is such a thing as "rock bottom" I don't know where it is or what it means. When I hit the rocks, I discovered new ways to dig down through them. The bottom for me was when I finally quit digging.

I was stuck in a cyclical pattern that had me chasing time. Until my life became so chaotic that the pain of the problem hurt more than the pain I would feel in early recovery, nothing was going to change. When I came off heroin and meth, I was certifiably insane. I would cuss someone out one second and the next moment cry and beg God to stop the suffering.

Chapter 12

The Spirit Awakens

My time alone on the streets was fortunately short-lived in that winter of 2017. I spent less than a month aimlessly wandering the streets of downtown Salt Lake City, living in isolation from friends and family. I traded or sold anything of value within the first seven days. My wife and son were safe at her parents' home, but I was not welcome there for obvious reasons. I eventually even lost contact with Uncle G. He had always been the guiding light and example of righteousness who I was sure would never give up on me. He saved my life in Las Vegas. He taught me the value of honesty and integrity in all my affairs. He helped me realize I was talented, and that I had worth.

I had spent two years living with Aunt Kathy and Uncle G in their beautiful home where I converted to the LDS church and became a member of the ward they attended just minutes down a steep, paved hill lined with foliage. They live in an extremely wealthy community, home to some of the most successful families in Utah. Uncle G always had some wild surprise up his sleeve which made life exciting. He once came home and said, "Get dressed, Chris. We're going to go hang out with Mitt Romney."

We went walking around knocking on doors with Senator Romney. He was a great guy. Uncle G knew I loved this kind of thing. There is nothing wrong with wanting to meet successful people who are full of wisdom and great advice. The friends I made in this neighborhood taught me to have humility and be of service. It became clear that if I put my faith in God, the outcome would bring me peace and serenity. I might end up with a giant boat and a few dozen sports cars as well, but probably not, and that would make no difference to my well-being.

Uncle G taught me that having wealth is great, and there is nothing wrong with seeking to become wealthy. However, becoming rich would have little impact on how fulfilling my life turned out. That was the lesson these faithful people taught me daily. I had an epiphany one day watching these multi-millionaires serve the homeless in downtown Salt Lake City. This was, of course, a few years before I, myself, became homeless.

I experienced a miraculous transformation in the two years I spent with the Frees. The values and principles Aunt Kathy and Uncle G instilled in me helped me cleanse the shame and fear that had enslaved me my entire life. I lost the desire to use drugs and alcohol and lived life with grace and serenity for the first time. People who had written me off as a hopeless victim of heroin addiction were shocked when I emerged glowing with the light of Christ—the same Christ I mocked as an atheist before moving to Salt Lake City to go to treatment. I came to believe that only the power of God could be capable of restoring my spiritual health. I knew that my faith in God, my willingness to serve others, and my commitment to rigorous honesty were the armor I needed to wear at all times if I were to remain free from the disease of addiction.

Three years later, as I sat alone in downtown Salt Lake City trying to work out what happened, I began to panic uncontrollably. I was sick, my heart was racing, and it seemed no one in the world cared. My heart hardened. I was angry. My mom had abandoned me. My wife had abandoned me. Uncle G had abandoned me, and God had abandoned me. I was alone in the darkest corners of my own mind that night, a place I shouldn't have attempted to navigate alone. I fell asleep on a large freeway bridge that spanned the width of several train tracks. The bridge's sidewalk had short walls which hid me from traffic and kept me safe from cars traveling at high speeds. I decided it would be as good a place as any to lay down and shiver in agony all night.

I slept for an hour or two. It was probably around 3:00 a.m. when for some reason, I shot up to my feet and looked out past the bridge. "I am going to kill myself," I thought. I meant it. I didn't think about my son, or my wife, or my mom, or Uncle G. I just wanted the nightmare to end. To this day, I don't know what stopped me from jumping. In fact, sometimes when I think back on that night, I struggle because I am pretty sure I made the decision to jump and put my body into motion.

I cried myself to sleep, able to see things as they were for the first time in months. Everyone had warned me. Uncle G stopped helping me pay rent in a weekly motel and had given me an ultimatum which I ignored. I crossed a boundary. I was failing his drug tests. I was lying and stealing. Uncle G had to save my life again, but this time he would have to make a very hard choice. He had to let me fail. Alone.

We hear those who have near-death experiences make claims that their life flashed before their eyes in what they believed were their final moments of life on Earth. With my legs dangling from the bridge railing, I looked down where, through a thin layer of fog, I could see a large zone with tributaries of train tracks covering a big open slab of land west of I-15. The sounds of semi-trucks steadily grew louder from where they first appeared on the horizon, eventually peaking in volume as they passed underneath me every few minutes. Even further down below, a long train fastened to the main tracks was passing under the freeway. The endless chain of tiny train cars seen from my high vantage point hypnotized me, and when the night finally became quiet again, I had grown calmer. I found myself considering the unintended consequences my suicide would have on my son, my wife, my parents, and Uncle G.

For the first time in my entire life, I was completely honest with myself. I knew exactly what I was and what I was not. I could clearly see that even after experiencing the miracles in my Recovery, I still had not addressed the issues causing my life to violently collide with misfortune. I had accomplished so much in those few years. I had converted to the LDS church. I married again and had become a father. I had begun to rebuild my finances after literally going bankrupt. I had a lot to lose.

I struggled with depression and anxiety my entire life and had been self-medicating as a result for as long as I could remember. After my divorce in 2008, I sought help for the first time as the result of a nervous breakdown. At 29 years old, I finally decided to seek treatment for my symptoms, willing to admit I could not fix this by myself. I was diagnosed with Bi-Polar 2 and Generalized Anxiety Disorder. Even mild emotions are hard to manage with these two monkeys on your back. The intense despair I felt would likely be the straw that broke the camel's back for me.

I thought of my first wife and how the affair that ended our marriage impacted me. I still had some self-esteem issues, and even today have a hard time trusting others enough to be vulnerable. There was a time when I told people that this one event turned me into a heroin addict. I really believed it too.

Monica, who is my wife today, could not help me that night. She was living with her parents, and they objected to my addiction. She and I had been fighting badly and I was feeling a lot of abandonment and loneliness again. I wondered if relationship discord was at the core of my addiction issues. I was getting closer, but the situation was actually the other way around.

There was something much deeper, more embarrassing, and more nefarious than everything else I had ever considered. The realization hit me like two tons of salami as it entered my mind. "Oh my gosh, please tell me this is not true?" I thought to myself in disbelief, hoping that I could dismiss the idea just as quickly as I had welcomed it. "I have a personality disorder, don't I?"

I was talking to God now, I think. "I have narcissistic personality disorder, don't I?" I was catastrophizing a bit, but I had the gist of it right. I am a self-centered and selfish person, and I will look for situations where it's easy to let others enable my bad habits unless I frequently remind myself not to. This behavior, created out of low self-esteem, was buried under layers of shame and codependency.

☼ ☼ ☼ ☼

Daylight arrived, and traffic was picking up on the streets. I wandered, looking for a phone. People wearing looks of pity and disgust watched me as they passed by. I realized I should probably stop having this conversation with myself in public because I likely looked like a crazy homeless person. "Wait? I am a homeless person." Something about this thought caused me to burst out with uncontrollable laughter. The harder I laughed, the more disturbed I probably appeared to people passing by on their morning commute. The terrified looks from spectators who were locking doors and rolling up windows confirmed this was true. "Oh boy, you need to get off these streets, Chris. You need to ask for help."

I didn't have a phone, and there was no money in my wallet. I'd been wearing the same clothes for days and gone just as long without a shower. My hair was greasy, my beard overgrown and unkempt. I was chased off the grounds of convenience stores and fast-food restaurants. I wanted so much to call my wife and my son and tell them I loved them. My life was a complete mess, but my experience on the bridge had given me hope. At least I knew I wanted to live. I still had some fight left.

For the first time in my life, I was able to genuinely acknowledge that I was and am powerless over drugs and alcohol, and that my life had become unmanageable.

When "Helping is Hurting"

by Gary Free (Uncle G)

C hris asked me to write this chapter sharing my perspective of our journey through addiction together and a little of my history.

Attending Granger High School in Utah during the late sixties was hardly the same as today. The term "drug addiction" or drug use was something I never really saw. It was mentioned when describing hard rock celebrities or something someone heard about happening at a party, partly funny but not at all the most popular thing in my circles. I never was invited to use drugs or alcohol. There was a mild warning always out there and certainly hearing about alcohol ruining lives was talked about. Sometime before turning 16, and not having a driver's license, I remember an evening with a beautiful sunset in the west and riding with a few of my friends on double-decker bicycles, freshly built in my friend's father's body and fender shop a few weeks earlier. We arrived at the entrance of the Drive-in Theater. Leaning our bikes against the wall of the shack, we paid our fee to a laughing attendant. We rode our bikes in and laid them next to the speaker boxes intended for the partially rolled down car windows. We got a lot of smiles from the couples in surrounding cars.

The movie was "The Days of Wine and Roses" with Jack Lemmon. Although the details are forgotten, I will never forget the feeling I had of total devastation for a newly married, young, successful, ambitious couple steeped in alcohol addiction; something I never thought about. It was a horrible feeling to watch and learn of the possible pitfalls of addiction. As far as drugs go, I never had any idea what would come to pass in the present day. The strength, impact, and availability of drugs has multiplied in ways that many people today cannot comprehend and now people, not understanding the complexity of the problem, unknowingly shame and blame the user, adding to the problem.

My nephew, Chris, my sister's son, had lived in Las Vegas, Nevada his entire life. In those days, we did not visit the Foresta family often due to busy lives and the six-hour driving distance. When Chris was eight years old, our family drove to Las Vegas to his baptism where I was asked to baptize him as a new member of the Church of Jesus Christ of Latter-Day Saints. That was a fun weekend, but truthfully, we did not know each other very well.

Years rolled by and we met each other from time to time, but I was not always sure which one of my nephews was Chris, Nick or Tony. They grew and changed so much year after year. Time passes.

I love my sister Carolyn very much and hearing about Chris being successful in his career was always refreshing good news. However, the good news eroded quickly. Things were looking very bad. The news just became worse and painful to the core. Numbness and sorrow followed me like a shadow. Soon, I had growing concern over a nephew I hardly knew. I could feel the pain of my sister for her oldest son, now struggling to hold on to his dreams, marriage, and even his life. Seeing this happen to Carolyn was one of the biggest challenges of my life.

The biggest challenge though was losing my 22-year-old daughter to a motorcycle accident. That was horrible. Losing someone to drug addiction is seeing death at the doorstep and feeling that you should somehow save the day. Personally, grieving the death of a loved one or the spiritual death of a loved one on drugs is something extremely difficult to endure.

Raising six of my own children was a monumental task for an ordinary guy like me. My wife, Kathy, made it work! Now in my late sixties, I was facing the new challenge of helping a once successful 33-year-old account manager who had fallen into the abyss and claws of addiction.

It was on a Sunday in the church hallway where I talked to a friend, Rick Dixon. Rick had a similar experience with his own sons. I learned that drug addiction was more complicated and painful than I thought. I told Rick about my nephew and he got me in touch with the Renaissance Ranch, a drug rehabilitation center for men. (Over the years, Rick and his wife, Christine, have been a guiding light during this challenging time for me and, of course, for Chris.)

One night soon after contemplating the pain for my sister and the possible end of the road for Chris, I felt prompted to call Carolyn and tell her about the Renaissance Ranch. I offered to pay most of the cost and to help get him admitted (Most of that you have read in this book already).

As I remember it—I called Carolyn and told her about the Ranch and how we could get him in. I warned her that it was somewhat Christian based, but that they did not force that aspect. There was a small silence and maybe tears on the other end of the phone call. She said, "You won't believe the timing of his call." She had been trying to get him into several places in Las Vegas but there was at a least a year-long waiting list.

I was happy and thought how great it was – he would enter and get better and the next year, he would bounce back to normal. What a great guy I was! And how wrong I was! My education about drug addiction had only just begun. (To date, it has been a seven-year process with multiple rehabs.)

Wondering if he would be alive the next morning and seeing him sweating and laying on the floor of his room during withdrawals, I learned that I needed to form boundaries, but at the same time, needed to be available. I learned that sometimes it was best to stand back and let him suffer.

I slowly learned that addiction is more than just a craving disease. I heard many say that addiction is a shame disease, and the opposite of addiction is connection. The temptation is to scold the person with statements like, "Why can't you just stop using?" or "How could you be so stupid?" I learned fast that shaming and blaming only adds to the problem. Walking the fine line between enabling and holding a distance and boundary are just very hard and never easy. No one sets a goal to be a drug addict.

At many points during this seven-year period, I prepared myself to accept the likelihood of an unwanted funeral, and in those same moments, needed to show strength and love. Love and connection are the keys to helping.

⚙ ⚙ ⚙ ⚙

Seven years passed and Chris had amazing highs and lows. He was near death many times, yet he rebounded to a life and hope he had never realized with a wonderful wife and an ambitious young son, ready for a drum set and music jamming with his musically talented dad. Life can be so rewarding and yet so distressful on the road to putting addiction in remission.

After a dark period when bridges had been burned and living quarters were difficult to find due to the condition Chris was in, a place to live was dependent on the trust of the landlord versus his lack of ability to pay rent.

It was late fall of 2017, and there was hope that Chris was going to get a new job and find consistency on his way back to Recovery. I (Uncle G) was once again in that difficult position of trying to discern, "Is my help really helping, or is it counterfeit charity where giving is just enabling that prolongs the day of reckoning?" I laid awake at night, said prayers, debated outcomes, yet could never see nor feel right about the choice of helping or withdrawing my help for a better outcome. I consulted with social workers, church leaders, my wife, and even asked for a special blessing of discernment from my ministers, Jason and JT, as to my role going forward.

I decided to help by paying the rent at an extended stay hotel on Union Park Avenue in Salt Lake City. For several months, I drove Chris to job interviews and sometimes counseling sessions. Our agreement was that he would submit to staying sober and to random drug testing. I arranged for a good friend to take the assignment of doing the drug testing. He was large and intimidating but could be as calm and kind as the best. I will call him Omar. He had been sent to the U.S. after service with the U.S. Army. Omar was diligent and confident in the assignment. Being large in stature, his friendship with Chris was not going to stop him from being thorough.

One Saturday morning, I was to meet them both at the hotel to drop off some test kits. We all three met in the room and it felt friendly and optimistic. Chris's five-year-old son had been there earlier and things were good—so it seemed. I was in a hurry to get to a grandson's soccer game, so I rushed out and down the elevator to my newly washed yellow Corvette. I no sooner started driving down the street when my cell phone began ringing. I pulled over and looked on the screen to see it was Omar. "Hello, Omar," I said, "What's up?"

"You must come back," he said.

"I'm in a hurry. I have a game to be at. Why?" I strongly said. The reply was stronger and resolute. "My Elder, come back to the room now!"

"Okay," I said.

I rushed back and pushed the elevator button, trying to think what the problem could be. As I knocked on the door, Omar opened it and there was Chris in the corner with his head in his hands, moving in a way that expressed anger. Omar picked up the cup of the urine sample and said to me, "Why is this urine and cup cold?"

Chris was now having fits, knowing that this was all coming to a head. Omar said, "My Elder, why is there an empty cup in the garbage? Omar had figured out that in desperation, Chris had stored a urine test sample from his son while disposing of the real sample in the bathroom. Chris was so upset and almost out of control. I could think of nothing more than to walk over and rub his back, and finally he hugged me. I said to him, "Think of it this way. This is actually good news. We know the truth and now we can move forward." Together we felt the truth of who he really was and the fact that - helping can be hurting!

This one incident turned out to be one of the turning points for me and for Chris. I understood that if I had administered the drug test, I would probably have been so happy to see a negative test result. I would have been blind to the glaring facts. That is the problem when friends and family try to "help". I recognized this enabling trap almost every family with addiction must face.

Chris and I sat down and talked about a deadline—a time when food and rent would no longer be provided. At the end of that period, if Chris were not employed or sober, he would be on his own. This seemed to fly in the face of all compassion and love. But looking closer, we both knew there had to be a point where he would need to pick himself up.

At the end of the period, Chris had not met the criteria. The decision was made. He now had no place to live. I picked him up with all his stuff and dropped him off downtown. He was now homeless. This was a hard but pivotal decision. Chris was willing, ready, and brave in the decision. While I felt like I was betraying him on the surface, inside my soul I knew this was risky but worth it. Otherwise, the cycle of shame would only lead down the same fruitless trail of despair. I realized that what I was doing was not helping.

Now today, do I think less of Chris for this most embarrassing moment? Absolutely not! He has made himself vulnerable to write this book and to ask me to share this experience so that others can find a better way.

I am reminded of that great passage of scripture in Matthew known as the parable of the Sheep and the Goats:

Matt 25:35: "For I was an hungered and ye gave me meat; I was thirsty and ye gave me drink; I was a stranger and ye took me in;

36: Naked and ye clothed me; I was sick and ye visited me; I was in prison and ye came to me.

40: Verily I say unto you, inasmuch as ye have done it unto one of the least of these my brethren, ye have done it unto me."

I have learned that Chris and the many like him are sons and daughters of a loving Father in Heaven who knows of the great worth of every soul. I cannot describe in words the reward of seeing how Chris went to his own Garden of Gethsemane in great pain and anguish to the point of not wanting to continue, and then found his way back to his wife and son. His belief in the atoning power of deity and the blessings it brings were only possible after the trials of his visit to the lowest possible human condition where he hit rock bottom.

We all have different trials and paths. We all have a divine future if we but choose it.

Chapter 14

My Experience, My Strength, My Hope

My wife, Monica, and my son, Mason, live together with me in Draper, UT. There were plenty of trials we encountered along the way that almost tore my family apart. My wife is one of the most spiritual people I have ever met, and I truly believe that her continued reliance on God was the glue that kept us together. Against all odds, we somehow turned our will over to a Higher Power, as we understood Him, and allowed Him to make the decisions for us. Our best thinking led us into jails and treatment centers.

Life is not perfect now. She and I still fight like cats and dogs at times, and when that happens, the negative emotions come flooding in. Instead of pretending like we can avoid that from happening because we are afraid of its implications, we get out in front of it. When we have negative feelings toward one another, we force ourselves to get them out into the open. We are brutally honest with each other. If she calls my bad behavior out, naturally I am certain she is wrong, that I hate her, and that I should just go get high because she is wrong. Still, I take her suggestion and sit in those feelings for a while before I act impulsively. It usually only takes a few minutes for me to see that she was right, that I love her, and that if I get high, I could risk losing this all over again.

Addiction destroys lives and tears through families, but when we talk about it, it loses its power. Honesty, compassion, and hope get me through another 24 hours of sobriety each day. That is the message of hope I want to share.

We are only as sick as our secrets.

Made in the USA
Las Vegas, NV
03 July 2021